Introduction

This book is a step by step guide on how to work with and heal one's shadow.

It is a tried and tested method on how to become aware of, observe and heal your inner trauma that you have been carrying for a lifetime or even from beyond this lifetime.

ENJOY!

Contents

Knowledge of the Shadow

Just like the 12-Step Recovery Programme that addicts have been using worldwide for generations to help them overcome their addictions, I am hoping to develop a workable and successful method to help people face and heal their inner trauma or 'shadows'.

I myself have been working with my own shadows for most of my life and can say with humbleness and pride that although there were times when my shadow completely overcame me, I have learnt to embrace every inch of what is me and I have found the key to liberation from the torment of this inner shadow. The 'key' to it all that I have discovered through my journey I have broken down into 9 separate parts.

I have chosen the number 9 as it is the number representing the end of a cycle. Once you work with and integrate your shadow you will see how a cycle of pain and suffering in your life ends and how a brand new life begins.

When I talk of inner demons or shadows, what I am referring to is the inner darkness that we carry, our dual aspect of the light that we carry.

Inside of all of us lies trauma that we are carrying mostly from childhood but also from other events in our lives. This trauma can also be carried here from previous lives.

The problem is that we are not aware of the existence of this pain, or trauma, and do not notice how it reeks havoc in our lives. Our pain gets triggered and we act out, generally in unhealthy ways which creates more of these painful situations and this is how the pain persists and grows within us.

There are various ways the universe tries to wake us up to the realization of this shadow and we will get to all of that later on in this book.

Why do we call it a shadow?

We all carry pain inside of us that follows us like a shadow. Think about how the sun creates a shadow behind you when it shines on you.

So think of the sun as your true self, your God aspect, your higher self, pure love....

This love is always shining on you, and as long as you are in this reality it will cast a shadow.

There will always be pain in this reality as it is designed to be a dualistic experience and that is why we came here, there is nowhere else in the universe where we can experience this duality. However, this pain can be transmuted and we can take control of it instead of it controlling us.

The good news is that we can heal this shadow. You can never get rid of this shadow, you will always be light and dark, but you can integrate the shadow into the light.

Dark and light is just the term we give to energy: negative and positive, painful and joyful.

Everything in this universe is energy and science will teach you that energy cannot be created or destroyed yet it can be transformed from one type of energy to another.

Energy is frequency which is named as such because of the frequency at which particles vibrate and oscillate.

The speed at which these particles vibrate create concentrations of particles appearing as matter and sound.

The higher the frequency the lighter the energy and the lower the frequency the heavier the energy.

Let's look at water for example:

In its densest, heaviest form water is ice. If you speed up the particles in ice it becomes water and if you speed up the particles in water it becomes steam.

Therefore the frequency is low in ice and high in steam.

The same is true with the dark and light energies within us.

The energy related to pain and suffering and that we refer to as the dark or the shadow is a dense low frequency energy.

We often say we feel 'down' because this energy can literally weigh us down. It is dense and can block us up disallowing the high frequency energy to flow through us. It can cloud the mind like a thick black fog and can cause depression and other mental illnesses.

High frequency energy or 'light' energy is just that... light. We often say that when we are feeling joyful we are feeling 'light', or that we are 'walking on air'.

When we transmute dark or dense energy into light energy we often say that we feel like a 'weight has been lifted' off of our shoulders.

When we want to introduce a joyful topic to a particular conversation we are involved in we say 'onto a lighter subject'.

But 'light' also means illumination. 'Shedding light' on a particular subject or situation means to bring things out from the darkness and into the light where they can be seen and ultimately understood.

In turn darkness also refers to the subconscious, that which is not seen, and light refers to consciousness, that which is seen and therefore known.

When we transmute energy from dark to light, we are taking energy from the subconscious which has been pulling the strings of our existence from backstage and causing us much pain in our lives and we are shedding light on it simply by becoming conscious of it.

Once we are conscious of the painful aspect, the shadow, we can begin to learn from it and understand why it is there and accept it as part of ourselves.

Acceptance is one of the key elements of the love energy and once we accept the shadow we begin to transmute the energy into a higher frequency and ultimately into light and love.

This is how we unravel ourselves and heal the shadow.

And since we are beings who are only one tenth conscious, it is quite accurate to observe that 90% of who we are is subconscious.

A lot of what lies in our subconscious is what is causing us pain and suffering in our lives.

So let us begin on our road to healing.

You have successfully completed the first step: 'becoming aware of the shadow'.

You now have knowledge of the shadow.

Welcome!

Exercise 1:

- Take a notebook and a pen
- Write the following heading down: 'My Shadow'
- Then proceed to make a list of all the actions and reactions you have made in your life that have caused unpleasant situations
- Be as open and honest as you can, bring everything to light
- Read over it
- Know that this is not you, it is your shadow

Acceptance of Light and Dark

Now that we have knowledge and understanding of what light and dark are, let us move into the realm of acceptance.

Nobody can ever be pure good or pure 'evil' (as some might put it). In fact, when it comes to experience there is no right or wrong. There is merely experience.

There are consequences for deeds us humans as a collective would deem as 'wrong' in this world. But believe me when I say that the prison of pain and anger that causes someone to perpetrate certain 'bad' deeds and the guilt and internal suffering that follow these deeds is worse than any man made prison on Earth.

Mandela once wisely said:

"As I walked out the door toward the gate that would lead to my freedom, I knew if I didn't leave my bitterness and hatred behind, I'd still be in prison."

There are many labels in this reality of right and wrong, but as spiritual beings let us not forget that there is no right and no wrong.

There is however light and dark energy within us.

Within all of us lies subconscious or unconscious energy and conscious energy. The one cannot exist without the other.

Within the dark, or subconscious, energy lies energy that is of a low, dense frequency which is our purpose to transmute into light energy.

We must remember to refrain from judging the energy as it is merely energy, heavy energy or light energy, low frequency energy or high frequency energy.

Once we begin to label parts of ourselves as 'good' and parts of ourselves as 'bad' we create a dangerous rift inside of our beings that further causes the growth of the shadow in the subconscious.

When we label ourselves as mentioned we create the belief within our subconscious minds that we are broken and unlovable and that we are not perfect just as we are.

The truth is that we are perfection just as we are.

We carry light and dark within us and the one cannot exist without the other.

Striving to be only a good person, a person of pure light, is futile and it will drain your energy and will cause more damage in the subconscious which means that one day when the pot can no longer hold the boiling liquid it will explode and your life will be turned upside down. This happens all the time to people who always seem to be surprised and shocked as to what has just happened.

Desiring only one side of something is like deciding that you prefer the sun and then vehemently denying the existence of the moon. Let's just say that if you did this you will experience intense disappointment and heartbreak every time the moon shows up. And it will!

Pain is there to teach us and to help us uncover who we truly are. And we are all returning back to who we truly are, albeit at varying rates of urgency.

Some of us feel an urgency to return 'home' and others have not yet discovered that there is a 'home' outside of this reality.

This place I refer to as 'home' is a place of pure love, oneness and peace. It is not somewhere in the distance, it is within us. We are not travelling anywhere, rather we are peeling off the layers of who we are not so that we can return home to who we truly are inside.

The oneness that I refer to above is also another term for wholeness: the ability to accept everything that is, without labelling, without division, without judgement.

Striving to be only a good person is the opposite of striving for oneness and wholeness. Firstly you will not be able to be whole because you are denying intrinsic aspects of yourself and secondly you will be unable to achieve oneness because if you deny your own dark side you will be vehemently opposed to the dark side of anyone you encounter which will lead you straight into the ego's game of judgement and condemnation.

Empaths typically are people who have integrated their shadow and they can feel into and recognize the shadow of others and will respond with compassion and understanding.

Accepting ourselves as a full package is essential in shadow work. Loving and accepting ourselves fully as we are is the only path to healing.

Love is unconditional, you do not say "I love you if" or "I love you but". Love is not conditional... anyone who has had children will tell you that.

First and foremost we need to love ourselves with the same intensity that we love our children or how our parents loved us or how we always wished our parents would love us.

Love is the absence of division.

This reality is one of duality... this is how it is designed. For everything you can imagine there is its opposite.

One aspect cannot exist without the other.

A battery cannot have only a positive end or only a negative end, we cannot have only a summer or only a winter, or only a dry season or only a rainy season, we cannot have a north without a south, an east without the west, a day without the night, hot without cold, masculine without feminine, up without down, left without right, and on and on I could go all day but I think you get the point.

Denying any aspect of reality would be ignorant wouldn't you agree? So why is it that we choose to deny certain aspects of ourselves as if we are not part of this reality?

We are very much part of this reality. It doesn't mean that this is the only experience that is real or that it is our default position, but we are very much inside of this particular reality at this particular point in time so we are therefore part of it.

The second step in shadow work is to accept all aspects of reality including all aspects of ourselves.

It is imperative to accept our light and dark sides as building blocks of the being that we are.

If you were looking at a building that was built using blue and red bricks and you decided that you did not like the blue bricks and decided to have them removed, the whole building would come crashing down.

This is how we need to think of ourselves, removing any of our building blocks would cause us to come crashing down. All the building blocks are essential and are there for a reason, even the ones we don't like.

There may be some aspects of yourself you don't like, but regardless of that, you need to love yourself unconditionally. Your child may possess behaviours that you don't particularly like but that does not mean that you love him or her any less. We need to love ourselves this way.

Remember that light and dark make up who we are as a whole.

Your shadow is there for a reason, not as a part of you that is wrong, or bad, or a mistake or as some sort of punishment... it is your greatest spiritual teacher.

Accept yourself as a whole being.

Enter a lifelong relationship with yourself today and accept that you come as a package deal.

Exercise 2:

- Take your notebook and a pen
- Create the following heading: This is me
- Make an old fashioned 'Pros' and 'Cons' list of everything that makes up your light and dark sides
- Do not hold back on your positive aspects they are just as important as the ones you perceive to be negative, be what they may call 'vein'... this is your chance to compliment yourself in the most sincere and non-reserved way
- At the bottom write "I am proudly me"
- Stick that list up on your wall or on your fridge
- Accept that this is the whole of you and you are perfect just the way you are

How to work with and heal the Shadow

In order for us to see where our shadow is causing the most damage is to identify patterns within our lives which are unhealthy.

How do we know if something is unhealthy for us? Well that is quite simple: It doesn't make us feel good.

When something is 'unhealthy' or destructive in our lives it carries a heavy, dense energy and makes us feel drained, or uncomfortable, or uneasy, or in more extreme cases depressed, or angry or even suicidal.

We need to identify where the unhealthy patterns exist and how they are playing out.

For example:

I met a girl who told me her story about never being able to attract a partner who is able to commit to her.

She seems to always end up with the emotionally unavailable.

I asked her to tell me more about her life story. It turns out that she entertained suicidal thoughts on a regular basis and had even attempted suicide on two occasions.

I pointed out to her, in the gentlest way, that her inability to commit to herself and to her own life experience was the driving force behind who she was attracting into her life. I asked her: "How can anyone commit to you if you cannot even commit to yourself?"

The pattern she was suffering from was attracting unavailable partners who were unable to commit to her. The shadow was her inability to commit to herself.

Once you have identified the shadow you can begin to unpack it.

Let us continue with this example:

As we furthered our conversation I urged her to go back to childhood and describe the love she received or that was lacking from her parents.

She told me of how her father had left her mother when she was young and never returned. She felt abandoned.

She also told me of how her mother was emotionally unavailable as she was dealing with her own pain and working two jobs to pay the bills.

It turned out that she had been repeating the pattern of abandonment throughout her life.

She had always felt that she was not worthy of love and attention and therefore had chosen to abandon her own life, subsequently abandoning herself. She was also repeating the pattern of emotional unavailability by only being attracted to people who are emotionally unavailable.

Once she could see this, it was quite easy to see that the 'shadow' that was following her was really just a frightened little girl, her own inner child, crying out for love and to not be abandoned.

I asked her to imagine embracing her inner child as often as she could, bending down and giving her the longest tightest hug and promising her that she will never leave her and then keeping that promise.

Once she has committed to herself, she will begin to attract partners who are able to commit to her too.

Let us look at another example:

I have a male friend who says he is incapable of feeling love, or that he is numb to it.

He is a self-proclaimed womaniser and enjoys appearing to others as though he does not care for anything and as though he has little to no sympathy or compassion.

This attitude has landed him in some undesirable situations in life and also has led him in and out of loveless courtships. However now he is feeling that he would like more out of life.

I asked him about his childhood...

It turns out that he was put up for adoption just after he was born and the father from his foster family who raised him was an emotionless dictator who drank too much and treated his foster mother as though she was a possession.

He never really became close with his foster mother as she chose to be as quiet and dutiful as possible so as not to upset her husband.

This friend of mine's pattern in life was his unemotional attitude and womanising tendencies that landed him in unpleasant situations and loveless relationships.

The shadow was his pain from being put up for adoption and being raised by an emotionally damaged man who treated his wife as a possession.

Once he could see this we could begin to unpack it...

The fact that he was given up for adoption as a baby made him feel as though in his rawest and most vulnerable form he was unlovable even by his own mother and father.

It had become ingrained into him to not show his vulnerability in fear of being rejected or abandoned.

This is why he was repeating the pattern of denying his own emotions and vulnerability and choosing to appear as such as this he believed protected him... when in actual fact it was repelling him away from any deep and meaningful connections.

He was also repeating the pattern of how his foster father treated women. Treating women this way was easy for him to do because, although it was hard for him to admit and it eventually brought him to tears, he acknowledged that he lacked respect for women due to the pain he felt of his own mother 'abandoning' him.

We could now work with his inner child...

We could observe now that his inner child was a lonely little boy who was afraid to show any form of emotion or vulnerability who was raised in a toxic environment.

I could now guide my friend to face his inner child as though it were his own son and embrace him and give him the love he so richly deserved.

I advised him to constantly embrace his inner child and tell him that it is ok to be vulnerable and to show emotion.

We also underwent an energetic forgiveness process towards his parents who gave him up for adoption and I helped him realize that giving a child up for adoption is not out of a lack of love but rather out of a lack of ability and resources to be able to give a child the best possible future. In forgiving his parents he could let go of his pain surrounding abandonment.

The most common childhood traumas are abandonment (also manifesting as rejection) and emotional unavailability of one or both of the parents.

These traumas exist in almost everyone.

<u>Embracing the inner child:</u>

Embracing ones inner child is one of the most important aspects of shadow work.

All the shadow is really, if we were to give it a form that we can interact with on an emotional level, is our inner child.

The shadow is your younger self in your formative years before adolescence. Basically whatever age you were when you first discovered that life is not just pure peace and love.

Just like any toddler who is not getting enough love and attention our inner child will throw a tantrum. And a small tantrum can escalate into full blown chaos.

All that our inner child is trying to achieve is to get us to acknowledge the hurt that was caused during childhood and to embrace the child and to commit to loving him or her eternally and unconditionally.

Let us continue with a few more examples...

The purpose of these examples is to equip you in how to recognize patterns and how to unpack the shadow aspect so as to transmute it into higher frequency energy.

With these next two examples, together with patterns, shadow and the inner child I am going to introduce a forth observation: the gift.

So we are going to encounter 4 observations:

1. The pattern
2. The shadow
3. The inner child
4. The gift

A woman is complaining that she is in an abusive relationship. In fact her last 3 relationships were abusive.

In this particular case it was emotional and verbal abuse but this can be relevant to any type of abusive relationship.

She said she had begun her spiritual journey in hopes to uncover why this is happening and said that she had recognized her pattern.

As we unpacked her childhood and discussed her family dynamics we came to observe that her mother was verbally abusive to her and her mother's mother was verbally abusive towards her mother and the same went for her great grandmother and that this was in fact a pattern that ran throughout her family history. This was a pattern that was being passed down from generation to generation continuing the cycle of abuse.

In this woman's case she did not have any children as yet, but the cycle of abuse was manifesting in her relationship with her partners where she was once again assuming the role of the victim experiencing the abuse.

As we unpacked things further we found that the verbal abuse from childhood, that she had come to believe is normal and is just another way of expressing love and that there is something wrong with her, was the reason why people treated her this way.

She intrinsically believed that she was the one in the wrong and that she had to be obedient and less of who she was in order to be loved.

We began to talk about how she treats herself. For example: how often does she make herself a priority, or how often does she speak up for what she believes in or set healthy boundaries, or how often does she nurture herself and take care of herself.

Naturally the answer to these questions showed us both that she did not take very good care of herself at all.

It also came to light that she verbally abused herself by allowing toxic negative self-talk to persist and infect her subconscious enough to really make her feel worthless to the degree that she did.

The pattern was the abusive relationships she kept manifesting and the shadow was her own abuse towards herself.

She came to understand, through this exercise, that abuse is not just another form of expressing love, instead it is a form of projecting one's own unhealed trauma onto someone else.

She came to understand that love is supposed to be healthy, love is supposed to make us feel uplifted and safe and that it is imperative to establish healthy boundaries as a form of self-love.

We embraced her inner child who was a scared and tortured little girl who was crying out for her loving arms of protection.

The gift:

This is the part where we acknowledge the gift that has been given to us through having these experiences.

Had it not been for these experiences she would not have begun her spiritual journey of healing and transformation and is now working with other abused women and helping them to heal and transform their lives.

Because of these experiences she has put an end to the cycle of abuse that was alive for generations in her family.

She had finally terminated the cycle of a shadow pattern running through her family lineage and in doing so had saved the next generation from experiencing this shadow.

She knew that when she would one day meet the right partner and they would start their own family that their household would be free from any form of abuse and she would teach her children from a young age about self-love and healthy boundaries.

These are the gifts she received.

Let us have a look at one more example:

I met a very interesting young man from the States during my travels in South East Asia.

He had just turned 30 and had been teaching English in Asia for the past 3 years and said that he had never been happier and more content in his life.

He had met a wonderful Asian woman whom he fell in love with and they were engaged to be married.

He told me that his mother had died when he was very young and that his father had thrown himself into his work and had always been hell bent on making a lot of money.

His father was always concerned with what the 'neighbours' thought of them and he always had to have the latest and most expensive car, he had to be seen at the most expensive restaurants and of course had to be wearing name branded clothing and designer suits.

His father never seemed to get serious with any of the women he brought home and eventually remarried a woman with whom there didn't seem to be much affection but she fit the 'prize' profile as she too was obsessed with her looks and what people thought of her.

She was also senior management where his father had been working and both his father and his father's new wife were successfully climbing the corporate ladder, which in this young man's opinion was merely "a heap of people you needed to step on".

This young man had always possessed an artistic streak and loved to sketch, but his father had shot him down from a very young age and forced the idea upon him that the corporate industry is the only way to make money and that he must find a good job at a good company and work his way to the top through diligence and obedience.

The young American had been in and out of corporate jobs since he had left high school and just did not seem to fit in anywhere.

He began to see himself as a failure especially under the continual pressure from his father to 'become successful in the corporate industry'.

He tried as best he could to cultivate success in that industry but explained to me that he just did not possess that gluttonous hunger for money that everyone else in the corporate industry seemed to have.

He told me that the whole hierarchy system saddened and confused him as he could not understand how people could treat one another so cruelly simply because of the titles they held.

He said that all he really saw around him was overworked, depressed people who secretly hated their jobs running around carrying out orders that came from people who held delusions of superiority who also secretly hated their jobs.

He said that they all continued with this lifestyle because they needed the money. He told me that he noticed how people would literally do anything for money often at the cost of someone else's emotional well being.

Money and power was the driving force behind this profoundly sick institution called 'the corporate industry' and this young man told me that he did not resonate with this way of living at all. He said he struggled to hold down a job and the energies in these environments used to make him extremely depressed and even aggressive.

He said that very soon he was being viewed as a failure or reprobate by his family and some of his friends who had become well adjusted to this sick institution.

One day at the age of 27 he decided to end his life because he believed he had failed at what he had been taught was 'life' and what everyone else was succeeding at. He had no money, he could not pay his debts and he saw no way forward.

One night he drank a bottle of neat alcohol and with it drank a number of sleeping pills.

He said one of his friends had found him and rushed him to hospital where they pumped his stomach and saved his life.

Upon returning from the hospital to the commune he was living in he saw something on social media about teaching English abroad and approached his father to ask him to please lend him the money to pursue this as somehow it felt right to him.

Knowing that his son would probably not survive in the society they were living in he agreed to help him start a new life abroad provided his son paid him back within a certain period of time.

And that is how he came to live and work in South East Asia. He said that working with these children had filled him with so much love and joy.

He said there was no hierarchy system that fed delusions of superiority, there was only camaraderie and team work.

He said he made enough money to live and loved his life, and he was telling me how much he loved his job which he considered to be more of a calling.

He said he sketched in his free time and even sold some of his drawings down at the local market on weekends.

He had fallen in love with his soul mate and was ready to start his own family with her.

I have always thought of this as a beautiful and inspirational story, one that will be with me forever.

His pattern here was striving to make a success of himself in the corporate world and continuing to pursue jobs that he knew were not suited to him.

His shadow was his feelings of failure and his need to prove himself to his father.

He had realized, only after moving to South East Asia, that the world he had come from was indeed broken and the people working and living in it were bitterly unhappy and the rates of suicide and terminal illnesses alone were evidence of that.

He said he realised only after being removed from that world and looking at it from the outside that there was in fact nothing wrong with him at all, and that the life he was living now to him was his ultimate success and was the life he had always dreamed of.

The gift he was given through experiencing his pain is rather self explanatory:

A promising new life in a well adjusted society, the joy of working with beautiful loving children and finding his soul mate and starting a family of his own.

He told me that he understood the concept of embracing one's inner child. He said that every time he looked at the children whom he taught he pictured that each one of them was his own inner child and he gave them all endless amounts of love and encouragement and never ceased to tell them that they could be anything they wanted to in life and all they needed to do was pursue happiness because their own happiness was all that mattered.

Exercise 3:

- Visualize your inner child, your young self, the tiny boy or girl who experienced the pain from childhood

- Visualize embracing him or her so tightly and give them all your love and acceptance and forgiveness

- Imagine them always with you and when pain begins to show up hold his or her hand and tell them it is all going to be ok

- When you go to sleep at night imagine holding him or her close to your body and whisper to them how much you love them and that the pain and rejection is over and that you will be with them and will love them unconditionally forever

- You can even put a framed picture of yourself as a child next to your bed and whenever you look at it imagine that he or she is your own child and send yourself loving energy

The Mirroring Effect

This is the part I have been looking most forward to writing. This has been my biggest realization in this life. I would go so far as to say that if I were to rename this reality from 'Earth' to something else I would call it 'The World of Mirrors".

It has become apparent to me from the research into these topics that I have been doing since the age of 17, so for the past 20 years, that Earth was originally created as an alternate reality that souls could visit to mainly practice and advance their manifestation skills, but also to experience a dualistic environment which does not exist outside of this reality.

The problem with a dualistic environment is that together with everything 'good', or high frequency, comes everything that is 'bad', or low frequency.

Since we are all souls made up of energy the problem that occurred was that souls were aligning their vibration with that of Earth and so were no longer a matching vibration to the higher realms and were subsequently becoming trapped here.

Souls would eventually be re-incarnating over and over again in hopes to raise their vibration or frequency but were entangling themselves even further in the low frequency web.

Unfortunately since this is a very dense frequency environment the moment we become conscious here we only becoming one tenth conscious and lose 90% of our memory.

Earth however is not a prison! One of the laws of this entire universe, if not the most important one, is that there is freedom to choose.

Every soul has free will since this is a free will universe, there is no such thing as enslavement.

Therefore this reality is designed to wake us up as to why we are here and what we need to heal in order to raise our frequency and return home.

The most powerful mechanism that has been designed and implemented into this reality to wake us up is the 'mirroring effect'.

Human beings are mirrors for one another.

Everything that is unhealed within yourself will be mirrored back to you through someone else.

Whatever you see in someone else you carry within yourself whether it is desirable or not.

If you are an angry person, you will find yourself in situations where you encounter an angry person or people, and you will either be triggered and dislike this person or people, or you will know that it is a mirror and that there is anger within you that needs to be healed. In this example the shadow within you is anger and it is using the mirroring effect to mirror that back to you.

Let us look at more specific examples:

Remember the first example in the previous chapter about the woman who was never able to attract a partner who was able to commit to her because she could not commit to herself?

And remember our steps:

1. The pattern
2. The shadow
3. The inner child
4. The gift

The pattern can be defined as:

The mirroring effect repeating itself until you see and heal your shadow.

Her partners who could not commit to her were mirroring back her own lack of commitment towards herself.

The emotionally unavailable people she was attracting were mirroring her own emotional unavailability towards herself.

Let us look at the second example:

The emotionally numb guy who had created a persona that was attracting unpleasant situations into his life.

He was attracting people and situations into his life who were mirroring his unresolved issues from childhood back to him. The loveless relationships he was attracting were mirroring the lack of love he believed he had received from his parents who had put him up for adoption.

Let's look at the third example:

Remember the woman who was in an abusive relationship who had come from a long line of abuse in her family?

The mirroring effect had been repeating itself to her mother and to her grandmother and to her great grandmother and perhaps even extended back into past lives.

Every time the mother would mirror the abusive tendencies to her child, the child would, instead of healing the pain, choose to project the pain onto their own child like two mirrors projecting onto one another.

The mother was mirroring abuse onto her child to illuminate the shadow pattern of abuse and the child was mirroring the innocent abused child back to the mother revealing the shadow pattern of the unhealed inner child.

However, in this case, she chose to look at her partner who was mirroring this abuse back to her and chose to witness the pain inside of herself instead of projecting the pain onto herself or someone else.

Let us visit the last example from the previous chapter:

Remember the young man who was in and out of numerous corporate companies taking on jobs that made him bitterly unhappy?

Not only were these 'cruel' people mirroring his own cruelty towards himself by believing he was not good enough and was a failure, but so too were they mirroring his own father back to him whom he did not resonate with on a values level.

Being triggered:

Let us talk about the most important element of the mirroring effect.

The one way we know that we are looking into the mirror is that we become triggered.

Triggering causes some sort of uncomfortable reaction. This reaction is caused the moment the reflection from the mirror hits us, or reaches our being.

Say for example you heat up a mirror and then pour ice cold water on it, the moment the water hits the mirror it will crack. That cracking is the uncomfortable reaction.

It is called being triggered because it is like a bomb being activated, following this there is an energetic explosion in your being... anything from a small quiver to full blown chaos.

These 'explosions' can manifest as feelings of discomfort, or sadness, or irritability, to anger and even to aggression.

The rate at which you are triggered and the degree to which you are triggered is determined by the amount of unhealed shadow you are carrying.

The mirrors and triggers you attract are directly proportionate to the amount of unhealed trauma you are carrying within yourself.

Let us look at a basic example:

A man works at his company where his boss treats him dismissively and is rude and arrogant towards him.

His manager's behaviour towards him triggers him into feelings of anger. He blames this feeling of anger on his boss and spends years hating his boss.

Upon further investigation he realizes he too carries this nasty and dismissive streak in his personality when he observes how he has been treating his wife and children.

The anger he felt towards his boss was the trigger, through the mirroring effect, and also the alarm bells alerting him to his own unhealed trauma.

The mirror does not always mirror something to you that you have done, it can also mirror back to you something that was done unto you by someone else that has left unhealed trauma in the shadow.

Let's look at this example:

A woman is surrounded with friends who she believes to be vein and self-absorbed, she is triggered and begins to feel apprehensive and distrusting towards them and slowly begins to dislike them more and more.

Upon further investigation she realizes that her mother was extremely vein and self-absorbed and she was carrying anger towards her mother for not being more attentive towards her and for not noticing the truly important things in life.

The truly important thing to remember here is that any feeling of discomfort, when confronted by a situation or person, whether it be irritability or full blown aggression is that it is a trigger and the solution does not lie in blaming the person who triggered you but rather in looking internally and healing the shadow.

Projecting:

Since everything is energy, the energy of what is mirrored back to you cannot just disappear.

There is only one of two things that can happen to that energy: it can be absorbed or reflected.

If we absorb what is mirrored to us it means that we are internalising it and using it as a tool to observe and heal our shadow.

However if we reflect what is mirrored to us back out again that is called 'projecting'.

Many of us will choose to project our unhealed trauma and pain onto others instead of healing.

Remember that this is a free will universe and we all have the choice as to when we will heal and raise our frequency.

Unfortunately many people are not aware of this mirroring effect and of their unhealed shadow that is ruling their lives. However we are in a time now where there is so much more literature and information going around on the internet that at some point everyone will be made aware of this in one way or another and then they will be able to make the conscious choice of whether to free themselves or remain trapped.

This is a free will universe of fairness and at some predetermined point chosen by the souls themselves, or on numerous occasions, everyone will be made aware of why they are here and about the importance of healing so that they can make the conscious choice of whether to heal or not.

Exercise 4:

- Take out your notebook and a pen
- Write out the heading: This is my shadow
- Make a list of everyone in your life who is causing you to feel triggered, who is causing you to feel uncomfortable emotions
- Underneath each name make a list of what actions of theirs are making you feel this way
- On the opposite side write down how you observe those actions to be evident in your own personality

Everyone is my teacher

Taking into account the mirroring effect, wouldn't it then be accurate to say that everyone is your teacher?

People who bring you joy are teaching you how to be joyful and people who cause you pain are mirroring your shadow and helping you to heal in order to experience more joy.

Our healing and the raising of our frequency is so imperatively important in this reality that souls have agreed, on a soul level, to help with this process by being mirrors for one another.

We have all looked into the mirror and we have all been a mirror for others.

These are the contracts we have made. Some of us will become aware of these contracts and others won't. But they exist.

Should we not then forgive those who have hurt us since they have played a vital role in our healing process?

How do I forgive you say?

Forgiveness is indeed hard, especially when there is no apology.

Forgiveness is actually quite simple, forgiveness is saying "Thank you".

Forgiveness is gratitude.

Say "thank you" as many times as you can to the person or people who have hurt you.

It does not have to be done face to face. Wherever it is done whether it is done face to face, over a text message, or while you are alone with yourself as you sit on your bed late at night it is just as powerful as expressing it verbally. It still makes an impact on the energetic field around us and most importantly inside of us.

The first few times you say "thank you" it may not feel as though it is making a difference because they are just words. But you need to force yourself to say it so many times that eventually those words reverberate through your being like a tornado of love and light. And believe me, in time, that will happen.

After enough repetition and practice you will find yourself saying it automatically almost immediately after someone has triggered you. You will become accustomed to being grateful to those who are triggering your unhealed shadow and subsequently assisting you on your path to healing.

Remember that everything is felt on an energetic level.

Words are extremely powerful and have their own frequency and are a powerful tool that we can use to manifest healing and joy into our realities.

Words are magical and can cast spells hence the word "spelling". Almost every single belief system or culture that has existed on this planet has used chanting as part of their custom or ritual. Chanting is repetition. Saying something once or twice or even a hand full of times is not going to make much of a difference energetically, but repeating it over and over and over again until you can actually feel the vibration of it is what makes the difference energetically.

That is why negative self talk is so dangerous because if you are repeatedly telling yourself you are unworthy of love, for example, it will begin to manifest as an energy in your subconscious and in your life. This is what causes depression and anxiety. This influence of negative vibration can literally influence the chemical reactions in your brain which causes the illness known as depression.

Being verbally abused and hearing negative sentiments being expressed about you and to you on repeat can also result in what is mentioned above.

However we can undo these spells cast upon us of the repetition of negative words by replacing them with the repetition of positive affirmations.

So too can we truly energetically forgive someone by repeating the words "thank you" over and over again.

We may also have difficulty forgiving ourselves. In fact forgiving ourselves may be the most difficult form of forgiveness there is.

We have hurt people too through this mirroring effect and we carry guilt and shame surrounding that which is also manifesting in the shadow.

Ho'oponopono is an ancient Hawaiian practice of reconciliation and forgiveness.

This practice is made up of a set of words which are as follows:

"I'm sorry, please forgive me, thank you, I love you."

When chanted and used in repetition these words have powerful healing effects.

If you are interested in doing some research go and do an internet search for a Hawaiian author and therapist named Dr. Ihaleakala Hew Len.

He cured an entire ward of criminally insane patients by using the Hoʻoponopono method. And what makes the story most inspiring and interesting is that he did this without ever meeting any of them personally.

Exercise 5:

- Put a picture of yourself in a frame with the words "thank you, I love you" written above it or underneath it. This will help you forgive yourself by remembering to be grateful to yourself for being your biggest teacher

- Remember that you are only here because you have low frequency energy to transmute and so does everyone else and keep this in mind when you read the words 'thank you, I love you'

- Write down the names of everyone who has hurt you and triggered you in some way, next to their name write 'thank you, I love you'. If you have a picture of them use that instead of just writing down their name

- Chant the words 'thank you, I love you' to yourself and everyone on your list as often as you can

<u>Integration</u>

Now that we are working with the shadow and healing the shadow and transmuting low frequency, or heavy, energy into high frequency, or light, energy we can begin to integrate our light and dark into our being as one energy.

Working with the shadow is ongoing work and it is never something that we fully complete.

When we have worked through what we had initially come here to work through we will leave our physical bodies and ascend.

Every day that we wake up we take on the responsibility to our soul to work with the shadow, but not only to heal it but also to integrate it.

We cannot deny it or get rid of it. It is all our own energy it's just that some of it is low frequency and some high frequency.

If you were in some sort of accident and you wounded yourself somewhere on your body, you would not just cut that part of your body off and deny its existence. You heal yourself because it is part of your body and it is part of you.

Such is the same with our souls, we cannot just cut a part of our souls away and deny it ever existed. Parts of our soul's energy had been wounded through certain experiences in this reality and the frequency has lowered and has become heavy and dense. We need to heal that energy not by cutting it away but by raising its vibration and integrating it back into the rest of the high frequency energy.

The key here is never to deny any part of yourself, rather you need to love every single aspect of yourself.

Love is the highest frequency energy and by giving something love you immediately raise the vibration.

Integration is all about integrating all parts of yourself into the whole.

The gifts that you receive through your painful experiences are what makes you who you are today so we can then deduce that without your painful experiences you would not be you.

Your painful experiences made you who you are just as much as your joyful experiences did. In fact when we are experiencing joyful and peaceful times we do not learn or grow much, we are literally just enjoying the fruits of our labours and we all deserve that. But it is in the difficult times that we learn invaluable lesson about life.

We all need to remember this when we think of ourselves. Because all too often people think of themselves as being made up of parts they like and that are 'good' and that they want to be more of and then they think of parts of themselves that are 'bad' and that they don't like and don't want.

We need to cultivate an 'integration' mindset that all our parts make up our whole. We need to integrate or 'harmonize' all aspects into one and stop seeing ourselves as made up of separate and conflicting components.

<u>Exercise 6:</u>

- Let's play puzzles
- Go out and buy a puzzle
- Say for example there are 1000 pieces in this puzzle
- Open the box and just randomly pick out 500 pieces and throw them away
- Now build the puzzle until complete
- You are either not going to be able to complete it or you will but it will have such a massive chunk missing that it will not make up a full harmonious scene as shown on the box cover

- We are like this puzzle, every piece is important. Every piece has its place. Every piece makes up the big picture

Loving the Whole

As stated previously. Love is the highest frequency energy in this universe.

We are here to love ourselves as whole beings and not as fragmented beings with broken parts.

We are merely made up of energy. Some of this energy is high frequency and some low frequency and we are here to heal and transmute the low frequency energy.

We need to learn to love ourselves completely and unconditionally.

If you wound yourself physically do you love yourself less? If your child wounds themselves do you love them less? No. So why is it that when we have been wounded energetically we tend to judge ourselves and love ourselves less?

Why do we judge others who have been wounded energetically?

Loving the whole is not just about loving ourselves as a whole but it is also about loving the rest of humanity as a whole.

We need to understand that this whole reality is made up of high frequency energy and low frequency energy.

Through our individual commitment to raising our own vibration so we raise the vibration of the whole.

That is why it is so important to heal ourselves because this is the ultimate contribution to healing humanity we can make.

We cannot heal anyone else since this is a free will universe. Everyone is responsible for their own healing, however we can definitely assist one another once we have made the mutual or collective decision to heal but no one can heal another.

Healing is our own personal responsibility and when we heal ourselves we heal the whole, we heal the collective.

Energy is all connected and raising frequency on one end of the spectrum inspires the raising of frequency on another end of the spectrum.

The more energy that is raised the more it will begin to pull lower frequency energy up out of its density.

Let us think of a glass bottle filled with water that is heavy and has sunk to the bottom of the bathtub. The more water we release the lighter the bottle becomes and will eventually rise to the surface. The more frequency we begin to raise the more the collective will begin to raise, alternatively the more we allow dense energy to stagnate and multiply the more humanity will sink.

Our own personal healing is the most important task we will ever carry out.

Gandhi once said: "Be the change that you want to see in the world."

Never have truer words been spoken.

Exercise 7:

- This exercise I want you to try for a day and if you can get it right for a whole day then push it to 3 days and then a week and so on
- For one whole day I want you to only feel love for everything and everyone around you
- Do not allow negative thoughts to prevail in your head
- Do not allow yourself to judge another even if they are being unkind, just smile and say the words out loud or in your head 'thank you, I love you'
- See everything around you as part of the whole and that every puzzle piece is there for a reason
- If you are confronted with any anger or pain just remember that it is low frequency energy that still needs to be transmuted and

therefore there is some healing
you still need to do within yourself
and that by doing that you will
ultimately contribute to the
healing of the collective

Opposition

Unfortunately as you begin to raise your frequency you will encounter opposition.

This is a chapter I wish I didn't have to write but the truth is that we live in a reality where as much as we have people around us who will support us we also have people around us who will want to bring us down. They do not even consciously realize they are doing this but because they are so stuck in their low, dense frequency they will try and pull you back 'down' into that vibration simply out of a fear of abandonment.

Let us look at this in more detail...

Being in a specific vibration frequency over a long period of time, sometimes even lifetimes, can become addictive.

Some souls have become addicted to their low, dense frequency vibrations and they want other souls around them who are also stuck in those low frequencies.

Anyone who has been an addict and has recovered or knows anyone in this situation will tell you that addicts do not like to be alone. Addicts will share their drugs with one another and form unhealthy group connections. Although hardcore addicts care for nothing except the substance they are addicted to they still seem to care for their addict friends and this is a co-dependency relationship of an energetic nature. Low frequency energies seek out other low frequency energies.

And since one of the biggest traumas from childhood is abandonment, this is generally the root cause these souls became addicts, due to this unhealed trauma around abandonment so they fear being abandoned by their friends too.

You will notice that once you begin to raise your vibration you will automatically drift away from people who are not only carrying low frequency energy but who are unable or unwilling to heal.

As you raise your vibration you will automatically attract and be drawn to other souls who are raising their vibration too.

This moving away from low frequency energy people will attract opposition.

These souls will become desperate and will do and say whatever necessary to keep you on their level.

You need to become aware of the souls who are in opposition to you raising your frequency and ultimately moving on.

Like addicts they are terrified of being alone and generally all carry a fear of abandonment.

These people are also generally rather judgemental as they are still stuck in a dualistic mindset of right and wrong, good and evil because they are in denial of many aspects of themselves or have labelled aspects of themselves as good or bad.

When you begin to raise your frequency you will notice you become less and less needy to have someone by your side and start relying on yourself to get through life and start to feel more productive on your own as opposed to as part of a group dynamic.

This does not mean you will not feel that all of humanity and the universe is one it just means that you will no longer feel the need for co-dependency attachments.

You will become dependent upon no one but yourself and if you do fall into a group or partnership dynamic it will be because you both or all add value to one another's lives through mutual contributions and assist one another in raising your frequencies together.

As you begin to raise your frequency you will attract opposition not only from those who are desperate to keep you on their level but also those whom you pose a threat to.

Some will see you as a threat because you are living proof that one can heal and improve their lives and overcome toxic, low frequency behaviours such as co-dependency or victim mentality. And this poses a threat to them because they are still stuck in those toxic behaviours and were comfortable there because no one could see through it to the truth that it is not who they are, and now they are confronted with you who basically sees through them simply because you have seen through yourself and this makes them feel uncomfortable and sometimes they may even become defensive or aggressive.

Say for example a bunch of you were placed in prison for no reason, you just one day find yourselves in a prison. You don't know why you're there, there is no way out and you know it is a life sentence.

After some time most of the prisoners will have accepted their fate and become accustomed to their new environment.

Yet there will be some who will spend every day relentlessly devising an escape plan. Some will tell them there is no way out and they are wasting their time. The ones adamant on escaping and being free will invite others to join them but most will say it is too much work and it will all be for nothing.

One day some of the prisoners will wake up in their cells and hear cheering coming from outside of those walls. They will look through their cell block window and see the group who was devising an escape plan standing outside on the green grass as free and liberated humans. The prisoners still stuck inside are either going to admire them or despise them.

There will be people who are going to admire your growth but also people who will despise your growth and you need to be grateful for that too. It is the duality of the world we live in, and if they are feeling emotions of a negative nature towards you it means you have triggered them and you are assisting them in their own journey and the choice is theirs to

make on whether they are ready to heal
or not.

Staying Committed and Humble

Now that you are on your path of healing, there is no reason to ever feel as though you are 'higher' or 'lower' than anyone else.

Looking down on others is a form of judgement and that, in and of itself, is low frequency energy and it is just going to give you more low frequency energy to work through.

But even more than not wanting to judge because it is low frequency energy, you will come to accept that all should be celebrated as part of the whole.

Everything that exists that is perceived to be low or high or good or bad is part of the whole and it all exists for a reason.

We must view all of humanity as our brothers and sisters who are on the same path as we are on. We may all be at different levels and varying degrees of healing our shadows but that does not make anyone more or less evolved than another. We do not know what has happened to another soul and what they have been through during all their lives and what it is that they are carrying and where it comes from so it would be extremely ignorant for us to make assumptions or judgements.

We may meet someone who is still very trapped in their shadow and appears to be very 'unenlightened', however perhaps they have experienced severe abuse and torture in a hundred of their past lives whereas you may have only experienced abuse in your last two lives. Or perhaps they could even be a soul who has chosen and agreed to come down to trigger you and therefore be a catalyst for you to heal and grow. Remember to always say 'thank you'.

If you want to become a healer, just remember that you cannot heal anyone. You can however guide them when they are ready to heal the shadow and you can give advice and even assist with energy healing but the reality is that everyone heals themselves when they are ready.

Please do not make the mistake of calling yourself a healer or a Shaman and taking the credit for healing people or becoming entangled in a hierarchy system.

Remember that we are all one and we are all on exactly the same level of importance and worth. No one is more important or less important than anyone else, no one is more advanced or less advanced than another, we are all here to heal, we all have unhealed trauma that we are carrying or we would not be here.

Last but not least stay committed to your healing and growth.

Every day we need to be cognisant of our actions and follow the steps of seeing the mirror, embracing the trigger, looking inside, finding the shadow, unpacking the shadow and healing it by integrating it and continuing to love ourselves unconditionally.

It is imperative not to forget that we are perfect just the way we are.

Stay committed and stay humble.

Let us recap on all the steps we have been through and the key elements to remember:

1. Knowledge of the shadow

   Obtaining this first step has often got little to do with your conscious decisions and more to do with your soul guiding you on a spiritual level.

   You are reading this book for a reason and all of us are at some point or another going to be made aware of our shadow.

   I cannot however re-iterate enough that this is a free will universe and every soul has the choice on whether to heal the shadow or not.

   However no-one can put off healing the shadow forever, we are all destined to heal and return home sooner or later, but the choice is ours as to whether it will be sooner or later.

2. Acceptance of light and dark

This is a crucial step in accepting ourselves just as we are.

Our light and dark sides make up the whole of who we are.

Wc cannot be all light and we cannot be all dark. We have to accept that we are both energies and that these two energies desire to dance with one another in harmony.

Acceptance is the keyword in this second step. Full acceptance of who we are is crucial to the healing process.

3. <u>How to work with and heal the shadow</u>

This step is where we find and heal the shadow by bringing it out of the dark and into the light, out of our subconscious and into consciousness.

This is where we liberate ourselves by observing and working with our inner shadow or what can also be called 'inner trauma'.

Here we worked with 4 steps:

1) The Pattern:
Becoming aware of the unhealthy patterns we have formed in our lives

2) The Shadow:
   Finding and unpacking
   the shadow that has
   been the driving force
   behind our unhealthy
   patterns

3) The Inner Child:
   Embracing our inner
   child and giving him or
   her unlimited and
   unconditional love

4) The Gift:
   Acknowledging and
   being grateful for the

4. <u>The mirroring effect</u>

This step is where we become
aware of the mirror that others
hold up for us.

This is where we observe how
everyone is holding up a mirror for
us in order for us to see what still
needs healing within ourselves.

We looked at what it means to be
'triggered' by someone. When we
are triggered by someone it causes
an uncomfortable feeling and it
has nothing to do with the other
person but rather is a sign that we
are carrying unhealed trauma.
This is a very integral aspect of
the mirroring effect.

We also looked at what it means
to project. When we project it

means that instead of absorbing what is mirrored back to us and healing our inner shadow we project it outward and inflict the pain upon someone else.

In this step we learnt how important it is not to project and blame others and to rather turn within and heal the shadow that is causing us pain and suffering.

5. Everyone is my teacher

Here we learnt that since everyone is holding up a mirror for us everyone therefore is our teacher.

We learnt about how important it is to be grateful to everyone and to use the mantra:

"Thank you, I love you"

6. <u>Integration</u>

Here we learnt how important it is to integrate the dark into the light, integrate and transmute the low frequency energy into high frequency energy.

We need to integrate all our aspects into one and not try to cut off or deny any aspects of ourselves.

I always say:

"Appreciate the light, and learn from the dark"

7. Loving the whole

Since 'love' is the highest
frequency in this universe, we can
heal all our shadow aspects by
giving it love.

Love is about acceptance of what
is. It is about the acceptance of
everything as a whole and
acceptance of everyone as one.

Loving every aspect of ourselves is
crucial. And once we can see that
there are no 'good' or 'bad' aspects
to us it is all just energy of varying
frequency we can love that
frequency and therefore raise that
frequency and ultimately heal
ourselves and liberate our souls.

Love the whole of you.

Love the whole of humanity.

But it all starts with you!

8. <u>Opposition</u>

It is important to know that although there will be people who will support our healing and growth there will also be people who will not support it and may even be vehemently against it.

It is important to be aware of this and to not allow it to divert you from your path of healing.

Love everyone who crosses your path and remember to say the words:

"Thank you, I love you"

9. <u>Stay committed and humble</u>

It is important to remember that the healing process is an ongoing process and it takes daily commitment and perseverance.

Staying mindful of how life teaches us and how other people are here to help us grow is of paramount importance.

Also we need to remember that we are all on our own, unique and equally important journeys that will one day bring us all back to oneness. No one is more or less important than the next.

We must walk our path with humble footsteps of understanding and compassion.

Thank you
for reading
my book:
"A Guide to
Shadow
Work"

Herewith a quote from my previous book 'Evolution of a Battered Mind' which is also available on Amazon.com:

"You can never be all good and you can never be all bad. Good and bad are just labels. You are an infinite flow of all things, of all emotions. You are light and dark dancing together in an illusory reality where the sole purpose is the expansion of your consciousness. All the terrible things that you perceive that have happened 'to' you and the negative emotions attached to all those things that happened all form part of the light shining in the distance atop a giant lighthouse showing you the way back home to unconditional love."

Love Yourself

Passionately

Made in the USA
Columbia, SC
15 January 2021